1374

D1650905

SLAP SHOT

Author

Bill Stokes

Photography

Melchior DiGiacomo

Heinz Kluetmeier

© Advanced Learning Concepts, Inc., 1975

Copyright © 1975 by Advanced Learning Concepts, Inc.

International copyrights reserved in all countries.

No part of this book may be reproduced in any form whatsoever without the written permission of the publisher.

Library of Congress Number: 75-22001

ISBN 0-8172-0236-6

Published by **Advanced Learning Concepts, Inc.**
Milwaukee, Wisconsin

A Product of **Advanced Learning Concepts, Inc.
and Follett Publishing Company**
A Division of Follett Corporation
Chicago, Illinois

Contents

1	**You Are a Hockey Freak**	6
2	**Thin Ice and Thick Skulls**	14
3	**Early Pucks and Eager People**	22
4	**Getting It Together**	30
5	**Skates and Sticks and Things**	40
6	**The Big Bad Bruisers**	48
7	**You and Me and the Stanley Cup**	58
	Pre-Reading Aids	63
	Discussion Questions	71
	Related Activities	72

1
You Are a Hockey Freak

Hockey!

The fastest team sport in the world.

You are in the game.

Ten people with sticks in their hands come at you all at once. They come fast, flying and flopping like a flock of huge vultures.

You stand alone on one end of a big, flat sheet of ice. There are steel blades on the bottoms of your feet, and thick pads cover your body. You look out through a white mask that covers your face.

The people coming at you wear skates and brightly-colored uniforms. They use their sticks to pass a small, hard rubber disk back and forth across the ice. It goes so fast you can hardly see it.

The skaters are almost on top of you now, still going full speed. Your insides feel like cold oatmeal.

Then one of the skaters hits the rubber disk with his stick. He hits it so hard that there is a sound like a gun shot.

Crack!

The disk comes straight toward you like a bullet. It smashes into your chest with a loud *whock*. You are knocked off your feet.

You try to grab the small piece of rubber. It bounces away and somebody else whacks it with a stick. It shoots past your arm and into the three-sided net cage in back of you.

A red light blinks on.

People around the edges of the ice shout and cheer. They are not shouting and cheering for you. In fact, some of them may even point at you and call you a "sieve."

What you are, of course, is a goalie in the wild game of hockey. The red light and the crowd shouting means that the other team has just scored a goal. Since you

are the one who guards the goal, that score is more or less your fault.

You do not feel so good. You wonder why you ever wanted to be a goalie in the first place. Maybe you even wonder why you ever wanted to be a hockey player of any kind.

But there is no time to worry. You have to get yourself set again because there is a face-off out there at center ice. The play could be coming your way in a split second.

You don't have time to think about the goal that was just scored. You just crouch and get ready to stop that puck of rock-hard rubber that may come at you at a hundred miles per hour.

Your heart pounds. The blood races through you as if it were hot oil. Your body is clammy and warm.

Suddenly the play is headed your way again. Your defensemen are skating backwards toward you. The center and two wings from the other team pass the puck back and forth. ZZZZZZZZip-Whack! ZZZZZZZZip-Whack!

Your teammates try to get the puck. They poke at it with their sticks. They throw themselves at the puck carrier with bone-jarring force.

But the puck moves closer. It shoots back and forth like a black bead of light looking for a hole to crawl into. You crouch lower and your muscles tighten.

Then there is a shot. It is a powerful wrist shot by one of the other team's forwards. You see it from the corner of your eye. You fling yourself to the left. The puck

thunks into your big, padded glove. You toss the puck off in back of the net to one of your players.

The crowd cheers, this time for you. You have made a "save." Behind your padded fiberglass mask, you smile a little. You feel good.

Then you know that there isn't any place you would rather be than on the ice in a rip-roaring hockey game.

You are a hockey freak.

You've got a lot of company. Nobody really knows just how much. About the time someone claims to know how many hockey players there are, thousands more take up the sport.

You can say this: Hockey players are thicker than snowfleas. There are hundreds of professionals, thousands of college and junior players, and millions of others of all ages whacking pucks all over the place.

2
Thin Ice and Thick Skulls

There are so many hockey freaks these days that in most places there isn't enough ice to go around. Indoor rinks are open almost around-the-clock. Still they can't serve all of those who want ice time.

Of course there is a lot of hockey that doesn't require a fancy, brightly-lighted indoor rink. There are parts of the world where the winters are so cold that lakes and rivers are frozen over much of the year. In such places the fire department can make a rink with a fire hose. More hockey is played on this ice than you can shake a white ash stick at.

Some people call this kind of hockey "shinny." It is played all winter long wherever there is ice and young people. It is the real grass roots of the game.

Grab up your skates and stick and come to the pond.

It is Saturday afternoon.

A pale sun is kissing the snow with cold, wintry lips.

You sit on a snowbank with the others and lace your skates up. Soon the hockey game is on. Everybody is shouting. Skate

blades flash. Hockey sticks flail the air and the ice. The puck sails up and down the ice like a bird. It hits R. J. Holt on the forehead, and he bleeds briefly.

Then the puck goes zinging past one of the chicken wire goals up toward the head of the pond. Billy Holman skates after it.

Suddenly the ice gives way and Billy bellyflops down into the icy water. It is spectacular. Water and ice fly as if somebody had dropped a bomb.

In a second, with great thrashing and splashing, Billy is on his feet. He is gasping and sloshing through the knee-deep water toward the bank of the pond.

Everybody yells, "Yeh, Billy. Yeh, Billy."

Then everyone goes and helps Billy pull himself out of the water. He is so cold he

can't talk. Little drops of water are freezing on his eyelids. His lips are blue.

"Run for home," somebody tells him.

Billy runs. He is stiff-legged and his arms stick straight out from his body like a snowman's. As he waddles up over the hill, somebody shouts, "Don't tell your mother."

"Ya, ya, don't tell your ma," everyone shouts.

But Billy's ma doesn't have to be told. When her son comes home she knows what has happened.

And, sure enough, there is a sign on the pond the next day. It says Danger Thin Ice. No Skating. And parked up on the hill where he can keep an eye on the pond is a cop.

Now, every hockey player on your end of town is more or less in the penalty box.

Of course in a day or two the No Skating sign mysteriously disappears. The cop goes back to his regular beat. And the hockey game takes up where it left off. But now the ice is thicker.

It goes on all winter. Bruised legs. Broken sticks. Lost pucks. Arguments, endless shouting arguments. Sometimes a fist fight. Gashed cheeks. Loose teeth. And getting home late for supper.

It snows just about every day. Every time it snows the snow has to be shoveled off the ice. The snowbanks get bigger and bigger. The skating area gets smaller and smaller. By late February you can almost reach across the hockey rink with your stick.

Finally the sun gets high enough to start melting the snow. It also warms the ice so that it turns gray and mushy. Then somebody — maybe even Billy Holman — falls through the ice. The No Skating sign goes up, and the hockey season is over.

It isn't exactly a Stanley Cup climax. But it is the way it goes in a lot of places. Maybe there isn't a lot of falling through the ice. But hockey for thousands of players is still a ragtag, pickup game in the schoolyard or on a pond. Or maybe it happens over in the empty lot.

There is a lot to be said for that kind of hockey. It is, after all, in such places that hockey began.

3
Early Pucks and Eager People

It is 10,000 years ago. Thick glaciers of blue ice are creeping across parts of the cold earth. You step out of your cave with your hunting club on your shoulder. There on top of the ice is a stone, rounded and polished by the glacier. Just to be doing something, you hit the stone with your club. It skids off across the ice.

Congratulations! You may be the world's first hockey player.

Nobody really knows how it all got started.

Early skating probably grew out of skiing. Skiing was first done in the Scandinavian countries — Finland, Sweden, and Norway — a couple thousand years ago.

The earliest skates that anyone knows about were made from the rib bones of elk and reindeer.

The Dutch people have been skating on the canals of Holland for over a thousand years. Skating came to England about 500 years ago.

Back about the time that Columbus was talking Queen Isabella out of money for ships, a game called "bandy" was being played on the frozen ponds of Europe.

Bandy was played with sticks and a ball. That's about all that is known about one of hockey's granddaddys.

One thing that is known is that hockey, as it is played today, developed in Canada. Some parts of it may have grown out of a game played by northern Indians. And a few of the rules of field hockey and maybe something from soccer were thrown into the mix.

The early hockey or shinny games were no-holds-barred affairs. They were much like the game played by the kids on the pond.

There was, however, one difference. Instead of using a flat puck, early shinny players used a wooden ball. Games were played on lakes or other wide-open ice areas. So a lot of playing time must have been lost chasing the ball. Somewhere

along the line, hockey players got the idea that a flat puck would be better.

The modern puck is three inches across, one inch thick, and it weighs five and one-half ounces. It is made of very hard rubber. Before an organized hockey game the pucks are put into a freezer. That makes them glide across the ice better. And it makes you want to get out of the way in a hurry if one of them heads your way.

In the first shinny games any number of people could play. Fifty people on a team was not unusual. These had to be some wild games.

The first indoor hockey games were played by students in Montreal, Canada. Teams were limited to nine players. By 1884 there were only seven players on a team. The seventh player was called a

"rover." Today's team size of six players came about much later, long after the game came to the United States in the late 1800s. A team now is made up of a goalie, two defensemen, a center, and two wings.

Teams play on a rink that is 200 feet long and 85 feet wide. It is divided by two blue lines into three zones. Each of the two goals is placed ten feet out from its end of the rink. The goals are six feet wide and four feet high. That isn't very big if you are trying to shoot a puck into it. But don't complain about that to a goalie. The goalie thinks a goal is as big as a barn.

For many years hockey was popular only in Canada, some eastern cities in the United States, and in some European countries.

Then in the 1960s and 1970s something happened.

Hockey began to grow, slowly at first and then faster and faster. Hockey clubs and groups were formed for young players. More and more high schools and colleges formed hockey teams. Indoor rinks sprang up all over the place. Many of them were in warm areas that never have any natural ice. And, of course, professional hockey came booming into new places.

And hockey just keeps coming on. It comes on hard and fast, like Bobby Orr's slap shot.

4
Getting It Together

Skating!

Fly like a bird. Turn like a bee.

Skating is the name of the game, hockey coaches say. You have to skate naturally in any direction without thinking about it.

Forward. Lean in the direction you want to go and dig in with short strokes of your skates. Once under full power, use long, graceful strides.

Backward. Bend your body as if you were going to sit down. With your feet apart, push off with one foot and then the other.

Mobility. You have to be able to stop, turn, and change directions quickly. The puck zigzags up and down and across the rink like a bullet. You must be able to follow the speedy flow of play.

You have to learn leg crossover turns both to the left and the right. You have to know how to do them while skating both forward and backward.

All good hockey players are good skaters.

Stick handling is the second most important skill for a hockey player. That figures, because the stick is what you use to move the puck.

The stick must become a part of your arms. You must be able to feel the puck with it so that you can move freely down the ice with the puck without looking down.

"Keep your head up," the coaches are always yelling.

The stick has to be so much a part of you that you can make accurate passes that whack solidly against your teammates' stick blades.

And, of course, you had better know what you are doing with your stick when it comes to shooting the puck at the goal. Otherwise you aren't going to make the red light flash on.

There are wrist shots, snap shots, flip shots, and slap shots. Each one requires a different way of using the stick.

Now, about checking. This is the most confusing part of hockey. Checking can mean just getting in the other person's way. It is one way you keep the players on the other team from doing what they are trying to do.

You can put a body check on a player who is moving with the puck. This means that you stick a shoulder or a hip out in the direction the player is moving. The player runs into you and is taken out of the action.

Checking is also just getting back into a position of defense after an offensive play. This position is usually between your goal and your "check," the person you are guarding.

There is also a poke check. It is done by making a sudden jab at the puck with your stick.

Checking is done all over the ice and all through a game. It is the major contact of hockey. It is very important to the game. You must know how and when to check. You must know what kind of checking is right.

While it may often look that way, a hockey team is not just a goalie and five players who skate about aimlessly and bat a puck around until one of them shoots it into the net. Each player has things to do and an area of responsibility.

A hockey line is made up of three forwards — a left wing, a center, and a right wing. Imagine that the rink is divided into three lanes the length of the ice. Each forward has a lane and usually tries to stay in it.

The center is most often the playmaker. The center leads the attack, passing the

puck to the wings as play moves toward the other team's goal.

In addition, there are the two defensemen. Their main job is to protect their goal. To do this they must stay between their goal and any attacking player so that the other team does not get a clear shot at the goal.

Defensemen in modern hockey also do a lot of playmaking and goal shooting.

During the three 20-minute periods of a hockey game there is free substitution. Units of forwards and defensemen go in and out of the game on the fly every two or three minutes.

Because of the fast pace of play, skaters must rest often or they quickly wear out.

Everybody knows about hockey's penalty box. That's where you get sent for breaking a rule. A minor penalty is two minutes long. You get it for such things as holding, tripping, interference, or hooking another player with your stick.

A major penalty is five minutes long. This penalty is given for high sticking,

fighting, spearing, or hurting a player deliberately.

There are also misconduct, game, and match penalties which put a player out of the game for longer periods of time.

There is also a penalty shot. It's a little bit like a free throw in basketball. Here's how you can get a penalty shot. You're headed for the goal with the puck. There's nobody in front of you except the enemy goalie. Then, wham! Somebody trips you from behind. Because of this, you get to move in on the goalie for one shot. The other players watch from the edges of the rink. How do you think the goalie feels?

Penalties are costly to a team. With a teammate in the penalty box you must play shorthanded. This brings on the "power play" by the other team. They

attack and you're outnumbered. This is a time when a lot of goals are scored.

The most important officials in a hockey game are the referee and the two linesmen. The linesmen call "icing" and "offside." Icing is called when a defending player shoots the puck across the blue lines and all the way down behind the opponent's goal line. Offside is called if a player skates into the attacking zone ahead of the puck.

The referee calls penalties and handles face-offs. The face-off happens when the referee drops the puck between two players to get the puck in play. It is the "jump ball" of hockey.

So, now that we know something about hockey, let's get on with the game.

Get into your gear.

5
Skates and Sticks and Things

Who wears a garter belt, floppy pants, and lumpy socks?

You do if you are a hockey player.

The uniform and equipment of a hockey player may seem odd. First there are the long johns and sweat socks.

Then lower leg and thigh pads, which are held in place by big, heavy, footless socks. These socks are held up by a garter belt.

Then there are shoulder pads, elbow pads, knee pads, and tailbone pads. Suspenders hold up your loose-fitting pants. You wear a jersey with a number on the back.

You'll probably be wearing a helmet and a mouthpiece, too.

Your hands and wrists are stuck in heavily padded gloves. Tape is wound around your legs to help hold the pads in place.

Then, of course, on your feet you wear a pair of skates. Your skates are the most important piece of equipment.

"If your skates don't fit, you aren't going to be able to skate with them," the expert points out.

"We beg people not to buy their skates too big, but they do it anyway. They think they are saving money because they will grow into the skates and get more than one season's use out of them.

"What happens is they put on a lot of extra socks and the skates are loose on their feet and they are helpless out on the ice.

"Then people say they have weak ankles. Nuts! There is no such thing as weak ankles. There is just poor-fitting skates that don't give any support."

Putting yourself on the ice in the best equipment can cost a lot. But gear for a young player can be bought much more cheaply.

"Younger players always grow out of their equipment before they wear it out," the expert says. "And so in most places there is a used equipment sale at least once a year."

Some sporting goods stores also sell used equipment.

Once you get yourself all dressed and padded and taped, you aren't ready for the ice yet. You have to have a stick.

Hockey sticks are made of white ash or rock elm. Layers of wood are pressed together. Some sticks are coated with fiberglass. The "lie" of a stick is the angle between the blade and the handle. The lie will vary. It depends how tall a player is and how the player skates. The blade of the stick should lie flat on the ice when the player skates with the handle in a comfortable position.

The stick's blade is slightly curved — no more than half an inch. That makes it easier for the player to control the puck. The blade is wrapped with black tape, which gives it a stickier surface and makes the puck harder for the other team to see.

A goalie's equipment is different. A goalie has heavier pads and a broader stick. The goalie's skates are designed to help stop a puck.

The goalie also wears a mask. For many years the mask was not popular with the pros. But Jacques Plante started to use a mask when the slap shot came along. Plante says a mask saved his life during the 1970 Stanley Cup playoffs when a slap shot caught him right in the face.

So, everyone all ready, it's out onto the ice. Unless you are outdoors, the ice you

slide out onto is artificially made. The first such ice was made in 1879 in the old Madison Square Garden in New York.

Artificial ice is made by sending super-cool brine through miles of pipe. The pipe is buried an inch or so beneath the concrete floor. When the concrete is cold enough, water is sprayed onto it and ice forms. Most rink ice is an inch to an inch-and-a-half thick.

And more and more of it is being made these days as hockey slips and skates into more and more places. The chances are you will find some kind of hockey not far from where you are at this very second.

If not, hockey will be coming around the corner any minute now. Maybe it will be big league.

6
The Big Bad Bruisers

You are a pro.

The game is hockey.

Chances are your front teeth have been knocked out. Several of your bones have been broken. And there has been enough stitching done on your body to make a suit of clothes.

You love it.

What's with you?

Well, it all probably started back about the time you were so small you could get a black eye from a doorknob without stooping over. About the time you started learning how to walk, your father or your mother took you out onto the ice and put skates on your feet.

By the time you started school, you were using a hockey stick and learning how to shoot the puck.

From the age of five or six you were in some kind of hockey program.

You played your way up through the amateur ranks — mite, squirt, peewee, bantam, midget, juvenile, and junior. You went through the struggle of putting on

all the equipment so many times that you lost count. You got so you could do it in under two minutes.

And you practiced and practiced and practiced and practiced and practiced. Day after day after day after day, you practiced.

Sometimes you got so tired of hockey that you didn't ever want to see a puck again. Sometimes when there was a practice early in the morning, you wanted to sleep like some of the other kids.

You got tired of the coach yelling at you. DO THIS. DO THAT. DON'T DO THIS. DON'T DO THAT. DO IT THIS WAY.

When you got bumped or hurt or cut, you sometimes wanted to break your hockey stick and never pick up another one.

But you got so you liked hockey more and more. You got better at it and you gained more confidence.

Ah, yes. The pros say there is nothing more important to a hockey player than confidence. Lose it and you might as well stay off the ice, they say.

Soon your family and friends and maybe even a whole crowd cheered for you when you played.

Over the years you started to think that you were pretty good. You began to think about being a pro. Then you started to work even harder at your game.

You skated and practiced until you thought your arms and legs were going to fall off. You might have gone to hockey school in the summer when your friends were loafing and having fun. You listened

to coaches and instructors. And, of course, you skated, skated, skated. . . .

At about age 18 you went into either college hockey or junior hockey. In the United States college hockey is more likely. In Canada and some other countries you probably played junior hockey, which is supported in part by the pros. College hockey is not well developed outside of the U.S. Many Canadian players come to the U.S. colleges for that reason.

As a college or junior player you were noticed by the pro hockey world. Scouts came to watch you do your stuff. You must have impressed them. When it came time for the pro teams to draft young players, your name was on the list. Suddenly you were a pro.

So, Rookie, all those years of hard work paid off: You've got what you wanted.

So what is it like to be a pro?

Rough.

Think about this. When Gordie Howe's mother saw her first National Hockey League game, her son fractured his skull. After the game she cried and said she hoped Gordie would quit hockey.

Gordie didn't quit, of course. He played with Detroit for 25 years and scored 786 goals. Then he retired for a year or so. When he started playing again, he joined the Houston Aeros of the World Hockey Association. Two of his sons played on the same team.

Being a pro is tough.

Everybody gets cut up. Sticks and pucks and elbows and skates draw blood like knives. It's cut, bleed, sew, and back in the game you go.

Ligaments stretch until they can't stretch anymore. Then they tear, and that's probably it for the season.

A flying puck breaks ankles as easily as you would crack peanuts with your fist.

Being a pro is routine.

A losing coach will sometimes make you drill and practice and do wind sprints until you are panting like a dog in August. And there is endless travel. One airplane after another, with boring hotel rooms in between.

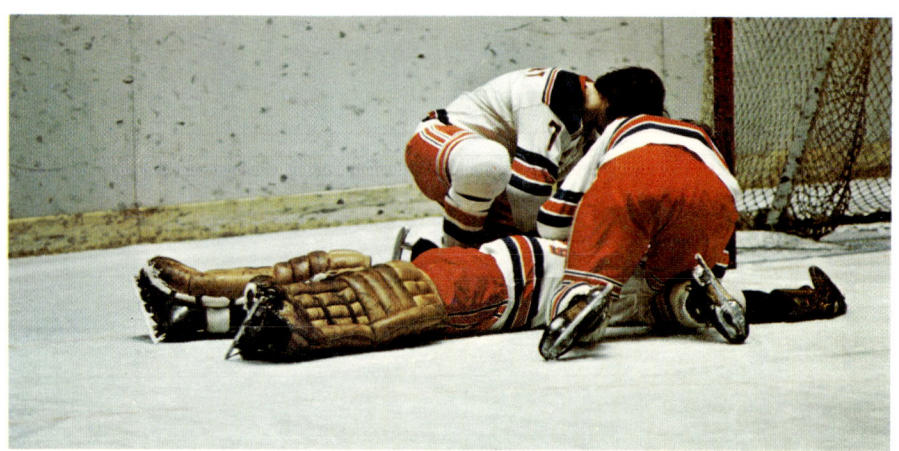

Being a pro is dumb.

Parts of it are. The stick fights especially. Grown people actually hit each other over the head with hardwood sticks.

When a couple of players whip off their gloves and go at each other, it seems to be an accepted part of the game. Some people think that's crazy.

Some people say crowds come to see fights instead of hockey. They ask, Why don't those people go to boxing matches instead?

Others ask: How do you teach young hockey players to control their tempers when they see the pros acting like street fighters? Good question.

So pro hockey is rough, tough, routine, and sometimes dumb.

But it's also money.

The money the hockey pros make has gone up like Fourth of July rockets. Hockey is getting more and more popular. More people play it in more places than ever before. That's why hockey players

make as much as players in other sports. And that's a lot, sports fans.

And being a pro is glory.

Listen to the cheers, but shut your ears to the boos. Sign the autographs and smile at the camera. Read the fan mail and talk to the reporters. Feel ten feet tall when you win. And let the excitement and warmth of it make the roots of your hair tingle. All the world loves a winner. You love the winner best if the winner is **you**.

7
You and Me and the Stanley Cup

You may play your hockey in a brightly-lighted arena with the crowd roaring in your ears. Then again you may play on a vacant lot. Wherever you do it, hockey is a game that gets inside of you and stays there.

Hockey has speed, drama, contact, excitement, strategy, and lots of competition. It is fun to watch and it is more fun to play.

Maybe you are already out there on your skates, or maybe you are just thinking about giving it a try. Anyway, it is time you heard about the Stanley Cup. Who knows, someday you may be on a team that is trying to win it.

The Stanley Cup is probably the most famous symbol of sports championship. It was started by Lord Stanley in 1893. Lord Stanley, from England of course, was the governor-general of Canada at the time. He became very interested in hockey. He put up $48.67 for the cup. It was first awarded to the best amateur team, but it turned pro in 1927.

At first the cup was nothing more than a battered mug about the size of a football.

During its early days lots of strange things happened to it. Once it was drop-kicked into a frozen canal by a celebrating player. Another time it was lost in a closet. And once it was left on a curb when the team that won it stopped to change a flat tire.

It has been stolen a couple of times, once even from the Hockey Hall of Fame in Toronto. It was recovered, however, and over the years it has been remodeled and made bigger. Today it is a huge, impressive trophy. You would probably give up your front teeth to see your name written on the cup. Many players probably have, come to think about it.

The cup is awarded each spring to the National Hockey League team that beats the other top teams in a playoff series. Competition for the cup may

eventually expand to include the World Hockey Association teams or even teams from other countries.

You don't have to be big to play for the Stanley Cup. Even in the pros there are players of medium height and build.

Hockey is also a game in which physical handicaps can be overcome. One pro — Bobby Clarks — is a diabetic. Another — Rod Gilbert — is a star in spite of having broken his back twice.

It is a game in which strange things happen. Bobby Orr, the best skater and player in the business, was introduced at an all-star game in 1973. As he skated out onto the ice to the cheers of the crowd, he fell flat down, like a kid who had never skated before.

It's a rough game.

Pre-Reading Aids

1
You Are a Hockey Freak

Purpose for Reading

What is it like to play goalie for a hockey team?
Do hockey freaks have much company?

You'll learn the answers as you read Chapter 1.

Important Vocabulary

You may find these words of help as you read:

vultures (vul·tures; vul′ chərz), *n.*
large birds with huge wings which feed on the flesh of dead animals

The cowboy looked up and saw three *vultures* circling overhead.

sieve (sieve; siv′), *n.*
a metal container with holes in the bottom which lets liquids and small solids pass through

Dad put the orange juice through a *sieve* to get all the seeds out.

face-off (face·off; fās′ ôf), *n.*
in hockey, placing the puck between two players from opposing teams to start play

The players' muscles tensed in preparation for the *face-off*.

professionals (pro·fes·sion·als; prə fesh′ə nəlz), *n.*
people who compete or do business for money

Don't play poker with Maurice and Frances; they're *professionals*.

registered (reg·is·tered; rej′ə stərd), *v.*
listed or recorded

Our poodle is *registered* with the American Kennel Club.

Pre-Reading Aids

2

Thin Ice and Thick Skulls

Purpose for Reading

What is "shinny"?

You'll find the answer in this chapter.

Important Vocabulary

These words may be of help in Chapter 2:

rinks (rinks; ringks′), *n.*
buildings with smooth floors for ice or roller skating

We couldn't go roller skating last Saturday; both *rinks* were closed for repairs.

grass roots (grass roots; gras′ rüts′), *n.*
the foundation or source of something

The mayor wanted to know what people at the *grass roots* thought.

flail (flail; flāl′), *v.*
to beat; to thrash about

You should have seen Billy *flail* around after he fell into the swimming pool.

spectacular (spec•tac•u•lar; spek tak′ yə lər), *adj.*
showy; exciting

The fire at the warehouse was *spectacular*.

penalty box (pen•al•ty box; pen′ əl tē boks′), *n.*
a place alongside the hockey rink where players who have broken a rule must stay for a certain time

John got five minutes in the *penalty box* for swinging his stick at Harry.

climax (cli•max; klī′ maks), *n.*
the most exciting part

The big battle scene was the *climax* of the book.

ragtag (rag•tag; rag′ tag), *adj.*
scrappy; unorganized

A *ragtag* bunch of little kids followed Cindy into the candy store.

Pre-Reading Aids

3

Early Pucks and Eager People

Purpose for Reading

How, when, and where did hockey begin?
How has it changed?

Read Chapter 3 to find the answers to these questions.

Important Vocabulary

These words may prove helpful as you read:

glaciers (gla•ciers; glā′shərz), *n.*
large masses of ice formed from snow

Much of Greenland is covered by *glaciers*.

developed (de•vel•oped; di vel′əpt), *v.*
grew; brought into being

The sport of hot air ballooning has *developed* since the early 1960s.

organized (or•gan•ized; ôr′gə nīzd), *adj.*
planned; carefully arranged

Millions of young people participate in Little League and other *organized* sports.

unusual (un•u•su•al; un yü′zhů əl), *adj.*
out of the ordinary; not common

It is *unusual* to see tulips blooming this early in the spring.

complain (com•plain; kəm plān′), *v.*
to find fault; to grumble about something

Don't *complain* about your hamburger; if you don't like it, ask the waitress to take it back.

natural (nat•u•ral; nach′ə rəl), *adj.*
regular; not artificial

Suzanne's hair has a *natural* wave.

Pre-Reading Aids

4
Getting It Together

Purpose for Reading

What makes a good hockey player?
What goes on in a hockey game?

The answers are in this chapter.

Important Vocabulary

Keep these words in mind as you read Chapter 4:

accurate (ac•cu•rate; ak′yər it), *adj.*
making few or no errors; correct
I think that Jody has given us an *accurate* picture of the problem.

defense (de•fense; di fens′), *n.*
protection
Everyone came to John's *defense* after Sam picked on him.

offensive (of•fen•sive; ôf′en siv), *adj.*
ready to attack
Jeffrey is one of the best *offensive* players on the team.

aimlessly (aim•less•ly; ām′lis lē), *adv.*
without purpose; pointlessly
We found Jane wandering *aimlessly* around the park.

responsibility (re•spon•si•bil•i•ty; ri spon sə bil′ ə tē), *n.*
duty; obligation
It is your *responsibility* to take out the garbage.

units (u•nits; yü′ nits), *n.*
groups of people or things
Three National Guard *units* were called in to stop the trouble.

costly (cost•ly; kôst′lē), *adv.*
expensive

Fixing the dents in this car will be *costly*.

officials (of•fi•cials; ə fish′əlz), *n.*
people holding public positions; people in charge

Many of the city's top *officials* attended our rally.

Pre-Reading Aids

5
Skates and Sticks and Things

Purpose for Reading What equipment does a hockey player need?

You'll discover the answer in Chapter 5.

Important Vocabulary These words may be of help as you read:

expert (ex•pert; eks′pėrt), *n.*
a person who knows a great deal about some special thing

Jeremy is an *expert* at fixing cars.

vary (var•y; vãr′ē), *v.*
to change; to make different

You can't live on hot dogs; you have to *vary* your diet.

designed (de•signed; di zīnd′), *v.*
planned

This hat was *designed* to keep the sun off your face.

artificially (ar•ti•fi•cial•ly; är tə fish′ əl ē), *adv.*
made by human skill or labor; not naturally made

These are not real diamonds; they are *artificially* made.

brine (brine; brīn′), *n.*
very salty water

Dill pickles are packed in strong *brine.*

Pre-Reading Aids

6
The Big Bad Bruisers

Purpose for Reading

How do you make it to the pros?
What's it like when you get there?

You'll find out as you read this chapter.

Important Vocabulary

These words may be of help:

amateur (am·a·teur; am′ə chùr), *adj.*
done for pleasure, not as a business or for money
Wesley is an *amateur* boxer.

confidence (con·fi·dence; kon′fə dens), *n.*
firm belief; trust
Juanita had *confidence* that she would win the spelling contest.

impressed (im·pressed; im prest′), *v.*
had a strong effect on
Joseph always *impressed* his piano teacher.

ligaments (lig·a·ments; lig′ə mənts), *n.*
bands of strong tissue that connect bones or hold parts of the body in place
Football players often tear *ligaments* in their knees.

routine (rou·tine; rü tēn′), *adj.*
doing the same things in the same way; ordinary
The producer wasn't impressed with the script; she said it was *routine*.

accepted (ac·cept·ed; ak sep′tid), *adj.*
approved
Yelling at the umpire is an *accepted* part of baseball.

popular (pop·u·lar; pop′yə lər), *adj.*
liked by most people
Motorcycling is becoming more *popular* every year.

Pre-Reading Aids

7

You and Me and the Stanley Cup

Purpose for Reading

What is the Stanley Cup?

You'll learn the answer as you read Chapter 7.

Important Vocabulary

These words may be of help as you read:

arena (a•re•na; a rē′ na), *n.*
a large space, surrounded by seats, used for contests or shows
The crowd went wild as the team entered the *arena*.

drama (dra•ma; drä′ mə), *n.*
excitement
We all remember the *drama* of that touchdown.

strategy (strat•e•gy; strat′ ə jē), *n.*
skilled planning
Bridge is a card game of *strategy*.

competition (com•pe•ti•tion; kom pə tish′ ən), *n.*
the effort to gain something wanted by others
Harold plays all kinds of sports; he loves *competition*.

symbol (sym•bol; sim′ bəl), *n.*
something that stands for an idea or condition
Our flag is the *symbol* of our country.

remodeled (re•mod•eled; rē mod′ əld), *v.*
made over
Our kitchen was *remodeled* last summer.

impressive (im•pres•sive; im pres′ iv), *adj.*
striking; worthy of attention
That certainly is an *impressive* ring you're wearing.

handicaps (hand•i•caps; han′ dē kaps), *n.*
things that put people at a disadvantage
A person who doesn't finish high school may have many *handicaps* in finding a job.

Discussion Questions

Chapter 1
What would you say to persuade someone to play goalie for your hockey team?

Chapter 2
Attack or defend the statement that shinny is the most important kind of hockey.

Chapter 3
What do you think is the most important change that has occurred in the game of hockey over the years? Why?

Chapter 4
A group of friends has asked you to explain what to look for when they attend their first hockey game. What will you say?

Chapter 5
Would you accept or reject the statement that hockey is not a sport for the poor? Why?

Chapter 6
If you were an official of the NHL and had to explain why the violence in hockey is not controlled, what would you say?

Chapter 7
Is the Stanley Cup worth missing teeth, fractured skulls, broken ankles, torn ligaments, and endless travel? Be prepared to support your opinion.

Related Activities

If hockey interests you and you'd like to learn more about the sport, you may want to do one or more of the following:

1. Write to: NHL Hall of Fame, Canadian National Exhibition Park, Toronto, Canada. Inquire about the following:

   when the Hall of Fame was opened
   what is contained in the Hall of Fame
   who can be elected to the Hall of Fame
   how someone is elected
   how many people are members of the Hall of Fame
   other information of interest to you

   Share your findings with your classmates. If possible, show a picture of the Hall of Fame.

2. Collect pictures that capture the feeling of hockey from sports magazines, newspapers, and other sources. Focus on a single theme (for example, the violence of hockey or the hard work involved). Display your pictures in your classroom.

3. Develop a chart explaining the hand signals used by the officials of a hockey game. Explain these to your class.

4. Make a diagram of a hockey rink. Include information about the boards, goalposts, nets, and the dimensions of the rink. Post your diagram in your classroom.

5. Conduct a poll of hockey players, coaches, and officials in your area. Try to discover how they feel about roughness. Do coaches encourage their players to be rough? Are players rough when they don't need to be? Do officials try hard enough to control roughness in a hockey game? Summarize

your results and report them to your class in oral or written form. Or, if you prefer, submit them to your school or local newspaper for publication.

6. Visit the library at school or in your neighborhood. Investigate what resources about hockey are available. Make a list of these, with a short description of each. Post your list in your classroom.

7. Make a glossary of hockey terms that would be useful to someone who is unfamiliar with the game.

8. Make a list of NHL or WHA team records. Include the following:

the most points scored in a single season
the most goals scored in a single season
the most wins in a single season
the most losses in a single season
the longest winning streak
the longest losing streak
other records that interest you

Post your list for the information of your classmates.

9. Using diagrams and other visual aids you create, explain one or more of the following to your classmates: headmanning, center rush, breakaways, power plays, face-offs, three-on-two.

10. Make a list of little-known facts about hockey. Include some or all of the following items:

the percentage of pro players who have had teeth knocked out
the location of the best seats for watching a game
the name of the first goalie ever to score a goal in pro hockey
the average number of hockey sticks used by a pro team in a year

the reason why hockey players avoid wearing the number 13

other facts that interest you

You may want to ask a librarian for suggestions on where to find this information. Share your list with your classmates.

11. Create a hockey corner in your classroom. Try to capture the *feeling* of the game. Display the results of these and other activities there. If possible, display hockey equipment, too.

12. Attend a hockey game or watch one on TV. Report your impressions to your classmates, using words, pictures, or sound.

13. Invite a hockey player or coach to speak to your class or school. Introduce your guest by mentioning the things you find most interesting about her or him. Be sure to send a follow-up letter thanking your guest for visiting.

14. Write to NHL Headquarters, 922 Sun Life Building, Montreal, Canada, and ask for information about the annual player draft. Explain to your classmates how the draft works.

15. Prepare a brief biographical sketch of Gordie Howe, Bobby Orr, or some other hockey great who interests you. Include pictures, if possible. Report to your class in oral or written form.

16. Create some cartoons, or make one or more comic strips about hockey. Post these on the bulletin board.

17. Visit the school or public library. Try to learn what the following trophies are for and who has been awarded each in the past five years:

the Art Ross Trophy
the Lady Byng Memorial Trophy
the Calder Memorial Trophy
the James Norris Memorial Trophy
the Conn Smythe Trophy

You may want to ask the librarian for assistance in locating this information. Inform your class of your findings. If possible, provide pictures or drawings for their information.

18. Make a Dictionary of Hockey Greats. Include the names of the best players of all time at each position. Provide a brief summary of each player's accomplishments. Include information that you think shows how great the player was or is.

19. Prepare a diary of a game official's day. Focus on the job: the work, the problems, the questions. What makes it worthwhile? Display your diary in your classroom.

20. Interview the team doctor of one or more hockey teams. Ask about the number and types of hockey injuries in recent years. Get the doctor's opinion about the dangers of hockey. Make the results of your work available to your class or school.

Reading and Curriculum Editor	Peter Sanders, PhD. Wayne State University
Associate Reading Consultants	John Clark, M.A. Cincinnati Public Schools Cincinnati, Ohio
	Ruby Cremaschi, M.A. San Diego Unified School District San Diego, California
	Edward Daughtrey, M.S. Norfolk City Schools Norfolk, Virginia
Story Editor	Maureen Reardon
Associate Editors	Deborah Gardner Nancy Mack
Coordinator of Learner Verification	Peter Sanders, PhD.
Related Activities and Vocabulary Sections	Peter Sanders, PhD.
Photography Editor	Eric Bartelt
Graphic Design	Interface Design Group, Inc.

Typesetting	Zahn-Klicka-Hill Typographers, Inc.
Color Process	American Color Systems
Lithography	A. Hoen & Co.
Binding	Lake Book Bindery

Manufactured in the United States of America to Class A specifications of The Book Manufacturers' Institute